GRATEFUL TOGETHER

GRATEFUL TOGETHER

a gratitude journal for kids and their parents

Vicky Perreault

ROCKRIDGE
PRESS

Interior and Cover Designer: Suzanne LaGasa
Photo Art Director: Janice Ackerman
Editor: Kristen Depken
Production Editor: Ashley Polikoff
Illustrations © Marish/Creative Market; Joel & Ashley Selby; All other images used under license from Shutterstock.com.
Author Photo: Courtesy of © 2019 Bella Iranitalab

ISBN: 978-1-64152-977-8

This journal belongs to

————————————————————

and

——————————————————————

We started it on

——————————————————————

Introduction

I'm so excited that you two have picked up this gratitude journal! If you've never kept a gratitude journal before, it's a place where you can keep track of things that you notice and are thankful for. What makes this one so unique is that you get to do it with someone you love.

This journal will not only help you feel more grateful, it will also help you feel closer to each other. There will be questions in this journal that you might not think to ask each other on an everyday basis. Sometimes my kids don't want to talk about their day or things that are on their minds, and that's okay. But a shared gratitude journal like this one helps us to connect even when they don't know what to say.

Whenever you use this journal, you will get a chance to express yourself and make your thoughts and feelings known. You will also have a chance to read what the other person has written, which is like unwrapping a special present.

Hopefully, writing in this journal is just the beginning. Once you start writing back and forth and sharing thoughts and feelings, you may want to keep doing it. You may even want to talk more about things you notice and feel. Keeping this journal together will be a great way to learn new things about each other while sharing the things you're grateful for. Have fun on this journey!

1

The Rules

This book features questions and prompts that will get you thinking about gratitude and each other. As you pass the journal back and forth, you'll each have the opportunity to answer the same questions and see each other's answers. If you are the child, your questions will always be on the left-hand page, marked with ME. If you are the parent, your questions will always be on the right-hand page, marked with YOU.

Before you start using this gratitude journal together, you'll need to set a few rules.

DECIDE WHO CAN SEE THIS JOURNAL

The two of you should decide if anyone else is allowed to read this journal. You may just want to keep it private between the two of you. Whatever you decide, it's important that you respect each other's trust and stick with it.

DISCUSS HOW YOU PLAN TO FILL IT OUT

You can fill out this journal in whatever order you'd like. Do you want to start from the beginning and work through from start to finish, or would you rather jump around to whatever entry catches your eye? There is no right or wrong way to do it. Come up with a plan that you both feel good about.

CHOOSE HOW YOU'LL PASS IT BACK AND FORTH

Figure out a way to let each other know that there is a new entry ready. You may decide to do this by simply telling each other, or you can leave the journal in a specific place. You can use a bookmark or ribbon to mark where the latest journal entry is.

SET A TIMEFRAME

How often you both write in this journal is up to you. Discuss the frequency that works best. You may decide to fill this out daily, weekly, or whenever you feel like it. Also, talk about when to expect a response back, and set guidelines so that no one is kept waiting for too long.

FEEL FREE TO WRITE ANYTHING

This journal should be a safe space where you both feel free to write anything. No matter what is written, agree that no one will get upset or in trouble. Also, make an agreement that nothing written in this journal will be discussed with anyone else.

Who made you laugh today?

_____

_____

_____

_____

_____

_____

Describe yourself in one word.

_____

ME

Who made you laugh today?

_____

_____

_____

_____

_____

Describe yourself in one word.

_____

Make a list of all the people you love.

_____

_____

_____

_____

_____

_____

_____

_____

_____

_____

_____

_____

ME

Make a list of all the people you love.

_____

_____

_____

_____

_____

_____

_____

_____

_____

_____

_____

Think of a way you can help someone in your family. What will you do? Who will you do it for?

_____

_____

_____

_____

_____

_____

_____

Think of a way you can help someone in your family. What will you do? Who will you do it for?

_____

_____

_____

_____

_____

_____

_____

_____

What makes your parent happy?

ME

What makes your child happy?

_____

_____

_____

_____

_____

_____

_____

_____

What is your favorite song? How do you feel when you hear it?

_____

_____

_____

_____

_____

What is the most delicious food you have ever eaten?

_____

ME

What is your favorite song? How do you feel when you hear it?

_____

_____

_____

_____

_____

What is the most delicious food you have ever eaten?

_____

List your ten favorite movies.

1.

2.

3.

4.

5.

6.

7.

8.

9.

10.

List your ten favorite movies.

1.

2.

3.

4.

5.

6.

7.

8.

9.

10.

Tell your parent something about yourself that they may not know.

_____

_____

_____

_____

_____

ME

Tell your child something about yourself that they may not know.

_____

_____

_____

_____

_____

What do you love the most about your parent?

What do you love the most about your child?

_____

_____

_____

_____

_____

_____

_____

Who is your best friend? How long have you been friends?

_____

_____

_____

_____

_____

Where did you meet your best friend?

_____

Who is your best friend? How long have you been friends?

Where did you meet your best friend?

List five things you are grateful for today.

1. _____

2. _____

3. _____

4. _____

5. _____

ME

List five things you are grateful for today.

1. _____

2. _____

3. _____

4. _____

5. _____

What is your favorite vacation memory? Where did you go? Who were you with? What did you like about it?

_____

_____

_____

_____

_____

_____

_____

ME

What is your favorite vacation memory? Where did you go? Who were you with? What did you like about it?

_____

_____

_____

_____

_____

_____

_____

_____

How does your parent make you laugh?

ME

How does your child make you laugh?

Use this free space for whatever you want! You can draw a picture, ask your parent a question, write them a letter, or tell a story. This space is all yours!

ME

Use this free space for whatever you want! You can draw a picture, ask your child a question, write them a letter, or tell a story. This space is all yours!

What is your favorite book?

What book would you love to read again?

ME

What is your favorite book?

_____

_____

_____

What book would you love to read again?

_____

_____

_____

Look around you. Make a list of the most beautiful things you see.

_____

_____

_____

_____

_____

_____

_____

_____

_____

_____

_____

Look around you. Make a list of the most beautiful things you see.

Describe an act of kindness you did for someone recently. What did you do and why? How did the person respond?

ME

Describe an act of kindness you did for some-one recently. What did you do and why? How did the person respond?

_____

_____

_____

_____

_____

_____

_____

_____

_____

You make me feel proud when you . . .

You make me feel proud when you . . .

_____

_____

_____

_____

_____

What is your favorite thing to do in your free time?

_____

_____

_____

_____

_____

Do you prefer waking up early or going to bed late?

_____

ME

What is your favorite thing to do in your free time?

_____

_____

_____

_____

_____

Do you prefer waking up early or going to bed late?

_____

List five things that you would bring with you to a deserted island.

1.

2.

3.

4.

5.

List five things that you would bring with you to a deserted island.

1. _____

2. _____

3. _____

4. _____

5. _____

Describe a time when someone did something to help you. What did they do? How did that make you feel?

_____

_____

_____

_____

_____

_____

_____

_____

ME

Describe a time when someone did something to help you. What did they do? How did that make you feel?

_____

_____

_____

_____

_____

_____

_____

I am thankful to you for . . .

I am thankful to you for . . .

_____

_____

_____

_____

_____

_____

_____

_____

How are you and your parent similar?

_____

_____

_____

_____

How are you and your parent different?

_____

_____

_____

_____

ME

How are you and your child similar?

_____

_____

_____

_____

How are you and your child different?

_____

_____

_____

_____

List ten things you love about the city you live in.

1.

2.

3.

4.

5.

6.

7.

8.

9.

10.

List ten things you love about the city you live in.

1. _____

2. _____

3. _____

4. _____

5. _____

6. _____

7. _____

8. _____

9. _____

10. _____

What are some things you do to show people that you care about them?

_____

_____

_____

_____

_____

_____

_____

_____

ME

What are some things you do to show people that you care about them?

_____
_____
_____
_____
_____
_____
_____
_____

What is your favorite thing to do together?

What is your favorite thing to do together?

Use this free space for whatever you want! You can draw a picture, ask your parent a question, write them a letter, or tell a story. This space is all yours!

ME

Use this free space for whatever you want! You can draw a picture, ask your child a question, write them a letter, or tell a story. This space is all yours!

What is your favorite food?

_____

_____

_____

_____

What board game or card game do you like best?

_____

_____

_____

_____

What is your favorite food?

_____

_____

_____

_____

What board game or card game do you like best?

_____

_____

_____

_____

List five things you like about your home.

1. _____

2. _____

3. _____

4. _____

5. _____

ME

List five things you like about your home.

1. _____

2. _____

3. _____

4. _____

5. _____

Think about the last time someone thanked you. What did they thank you for? How did it make you feel?

_____

_____

_____

_____

_____

_____

_____

ME

Think about the last time someone thanked you. What did they thank you for? How did it make you feel?

What is your parent good at?

What is your child good at?

_____

_____

_____

_____

_____

What is the best surprise you have ever received?

What do you want to be when you grow up?

What is the best surprise you have ever received?

_____

_____

_____

When you were a kid, what did you want to be when you grew up?

_____

_____

_____

List five things that you can do really well.

1. _____

2. _____

3. _____

4. _____

5. _____

ME

List five things that you can do really well.

1. _____

2. _____

3. _____

4. _____

5. _____

If you could learn another language, what would it be? Why would you want to learn this language?

_____

_____

_____

_____

_____

_____

_____

ME

If you could learn another language, what would it be? Why would you want to learn this language?

_____

_____

_____

_____

_____

_____

_____

What is the nicest thing your parent has ever done for you?

ME

What is the nicest thing your child has ever done for you?

Use this free space for whatever you want! You can draw a picture, ask your parent a question, write them a letter, or tell a story. This space is all yours!

ME

Use this free space for whatever you want! You can draw a picture, ask your child a question, write them a letter, or tell a story. This space is all yours!

What is the best thing about being a kid?

Describe a time you felt lucky.

ME

What is the best thing about being an adult?

_____

_____

_____

Describe a time you felt lucky.

_____

_____

_____

List three friends, including one thing you have learned from each of them.

1.

2.

3.

List three friends, including one thing you have learned from each of them.

1. _____

_____

2. _____

_____

3. _____

_____

What is your best quality? How does it help you? How does it help others?

_____

_____

_____

_____

_____

_____

_____

_____

ME

What is your best quality? How does it help you? How does it help others?

_____

_____

_____

_____

_____

_____

_____

If you could go on a road trip with your parent, where would you want to go? What would you do there?

_____

_____

_____

_____

_____

_____

_____

_____

ME

If you could go on a road trip with your child, where would you want to go? What would you do there?

_____

_____

_____

_____

_____

_____

_____

_____

What is the funniest joke you know? Write it down here and tell it to your parent.

_____

_____

_____

_____

What is something new that you learned this week?

_____

_____

_____

_____

ME

What is the funniest joke you know? Write it down here and tell it to your child.

_____

_____

_____

_____

What is something new that you learned this week?

_____

_____

_____

_____

List ten things you like to do on the weekend.

1. _____

2. _____

3. _____

4. _____

5. _____

6. _____

7. _____

8. _____

9. _____

10. _____

ME

List ten things you like to do on the weekend.

1.

2.

3.

4.

5.

6.

7.

8.

9.

10.

List three qualities a good friend should have. Who do you know who has these qualities?

1. _____

_____

_____

2. _____

_____

_____

3. _____

_____

_____

ME

List three qualities a good friend should have. Who do you know who has these qualities?

1. _____
   _____
   _____

2. _____
   _____
   _____

3. _____
   _____
   _____

What are three words you would use to describe your parent?

1. _____

2. _____

3. _____

What three words do you think they would use to describe you?

1. _____

2. _____

3. _____

What are three words you would use to describe your child?

1. _____

2. _____

3. _____

What three words do you think they would use to describe you?

1. _____

2. _____

3. _____

Use this free space for whatever you want! You can draw a picture, ask your parent a question, write them a letter, or tell a story. This space is all yours!

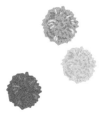

ME

Use this free space for whatever you want! You can draw a picture, ask your child a question, write them a letter, or tell a story. This space is all yours!

What was the nicest thing someone said to you this week? Who said it?

What is your favorite snack?

What was the nicest thing someone said to you this week? Who said it?

_____

_____

_____

_____

_____

What is your favorite snack?

_____

List your favorite teachers. What do they teach? What do you like about them?

ME

List your favorite teachers. What did they teach? What did you like about them?

What are you better at now than you were a year ago? Why do you think you have improved?

_____

_____

_____

_____

_____

_____

_____

_____

What are you better at now than you were a year ago? Why do you think you have improved?

_____

_____

_____

_____

_____

_____

_____

How did your parent help you today?

ME

How did your child help you today?

What is your favorite subject in school?

_____

_____

_____

_____

What is the best thing that has ever happened to you?

_____

_____

_____

_____

What was your favorite subject in school when you were the age your child is now?

_____

_____

_____

_____

What is the best thing that has ever happened to you?

_____

_____

_____

_____

List ten of your favorite things found in nature.

1.

2.

3.

4.

5.

6.

7.

8.

9.

10.

ME

List ten of your favorite things found in nature.

1. _____

2. _____

3. _____

4. _____

5. _____

6. _____

7. _____

8. _____

9. _____

10. _____

What are some of your favorite family traditions? Are there any new traditions you would like to start?

What are some of your favorite family traditions? Are there any new traditions you would like to start?

_____

_____

_____

_____

_____

_____

_____

_____

_____

_____

What is something your parent does that makes you feel loved?

ME

What is something your child does that makes you feel loved?

_____

_____

_____

_____

_____

_____

Use this free space for whatever you want! You can draw a picture, ask your parent a question, write them a letter, or tell a story. This space is all yours!

ME

Use this free space for whatever you want! You can draw a picture, ask your child a question, write them a letter, or tell a story. This space is all yours!

What is your favorite animal? Why?

_____

_____

_____

_____

Where would you like to travel to someday?
Why do you want to go there?

_____

_____

_____

_____

ME

What is your favorite animal? Why?

_____

_____

_____

_____

Where would you like to travel to someday? Why do you want to go there?

_____

_____

_____

_____

List five kind things you can do for your parent.

1. ______________________

2. ______________________

3. ______________________

4. ______________________

5. ______________________

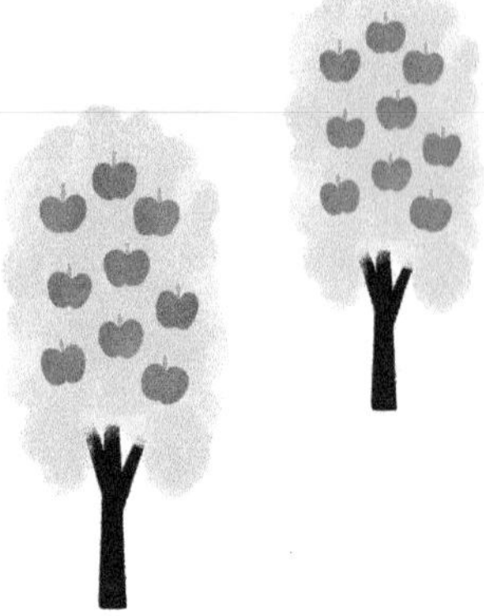

List five kind things you can do for your child.

1.

2.

3.

4.

5.

What is something you hope will happen in the future? How will you feel if it does?

_____

_____

_____

_____

_____

_____

_____

_____

ME

What is something you hope will happen in the future? How will you feel if it does?

_____

_____

_____

_____

_____

_____

_____

_____

What is the funniest thing your parent has ever said or done?

What is the funniest thing your child has ever said or done?

_____

_____

_____

_____

_____

_____

_____

Who is your favorite character from a book or movie? What do you like about them?

_____

_____

_____

_____

What do you like to do with your best friend?

_____

_____

_____

_____

ME

Who is your favorite character from a book or movie? What do you like about them?

_____

_____

_____

_____

What do you like to do with your best friend?

_____

_____

_____

_____

List ten things you like about the current season.

1. _____

2. _____

3. _____

4. _____

5. _____

6. _____

7. _____

8. _____

9. _____

10. _____

List ten things you like about the current season.

1.

2.

3.

4.

5.

6.

7.

8.

9.

10.

If someone wrote a book about you, what would the title be? What kind of book would it be—adventure, mystery, comedy, or something else?

_____

_____

_____

_____

_____

_____

ME

If someone wrote a book about you, what would the title be? What kind of book would it be—adventure, mystery, comedy, or something else?

What is something you would like your parent to teach you?

_____

_____

_____

_____

_____

_____

_____

ME

What is something you would like your child to teach you?

Use this free space for whatever you want! You can draw a picture, ask your parent a question, write them a letter, or tell a story. This space is all yours!

ME

Use this free space for whatever you want! You can draw a picture, ask your child a question, write them a letter, or tell a story. This space is all yours!

What is your favorite memory?

_____

_____

_____

_____

What do you think you will be doing in ten years?

_____

_____

_____

_____

_____

ME

What is your favorite memory?

_____

_____

_____

_____

What do you think you will be doing in ten years?

_____

_____

_____

_____

List five things about yourself that you feel proud of.

1. _____

2. _____

3. _____

4. _____

5. _____

ME

List five things about yourself that you feel proud of.

1.

2.

3.

4.

5.

What is the most important thing your parent has taught you?

_____

_____

_____

_____

_____

_____

_____

_____

What is the most important thing your child has taught you?

About the Author

Vicky Perreault is the founder of Mess for Less (messforless.net), where she shares kids' activities, parenting tips, and family-friendly recipes. She is a former teacher who holds a master's degree in early childhood and elementary education. She uses that experience to create fun learning opportunities for her children and blog readers. Vicky is the mom of three amazing girls and the wife of the best husband anyone could ask for. She is grateful for them all.

CPSIA information can be obtained
at www.ICGtesting.com
Printed in the USA
BVHW091829091120
592861BV00005B/5